Drives around EDINBURGH

Raymond Lamont-Brown

MACDONALD PUBLISHERS
EDINBURGH

Published by Macdonald Publishers
             Edgefield Road
             Loanhead
             Midlothian EH20 9SY

ISBN 0 904265 84 6

Cover design by Pat Macdonald
Maps by Hamish Gordon
Illustrations by Iain Mackinlay
Cover picture of the
Forth Road Bridge by
Stanley Jamieson

Printed in Scotland by Macdonald Printers (Edinburgh) Ltd
             Edgefield Road
             Loanhead
             Midlothian EH20 9SY

Contents

Come forth, the sky is wide and it is a far cry to the world's end . . . There is a road which leads to the moon and the Great Waters . . . and it has no end; but it is a fine road, a braw road — who will follow it? . . .

'The Rime of True Thomas'
JOHN BUCHAN (1875-1940), 1st Baron
Tweedsmuir, in The Moon Endureth.

Enjoying This Book

The nine drives set out in this book have a twofold appeal. They offer the motor tourist a taste of both the wild mountain, moor and loch scenery of which Scotland is justly proud, and the less spectacular, but uniquely beautiful lowland landscapes, with their strong literary interest and romantic flavours. Both of these are in stark contrast with the industrial areas concentrated on the southern margins of the Forth, and along the southern coast of Fife.

The tourist details of towns and villages, and the sketch maps, are meant as a skeleton on which the motorist and his passengers can hang the enjoyment of a unique area of Europe. All along the routes there are suitable places for picnics and historical centres should the visitors wish to explore on foot the local countryside or towns.

A quantity of minor roads have been included in these drives so that the visitor can savour all the aspects of the chosen area. Things to look for that are intriguing or curious are a matter of personal choice; but curiosities chosen herein are meant to reflect the character of the areas in which they occur. Whatever time of year the tourist may choose, the grandeur of the hillsides and the beauty of the plains and vales can be enjoyed along the routes of the drives.

May happy and safe motoring be yours along the road.

St Andrews   RAYMOND LAMONT-BROWN
July, 1982

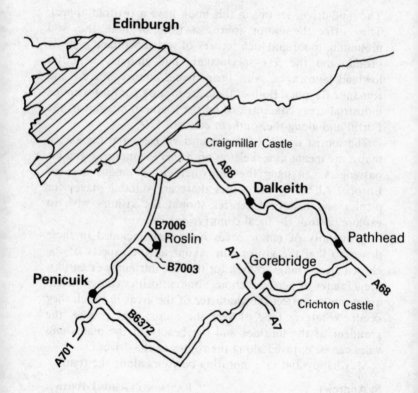

Edinburgh

Craigmillar Castle

A68

Dalkeith

B7006

Roslin

Pathhead

B7003

A7

Gorebridge

Penicuik

A68

B6372

Crichton Castle

A7

A701

Scale approximately 4 miles to 1 inch

1 Edinburgh — Craigmillar Castle — Dalkeith — Pathhead — Crichton — Gorebridge — Penicuik — Roslin — Edinburgh (37 miles)

A pleasant easy run through agricultural and moorland country, which has changed little since the Roman surveyors planned their major road of Dere Street to the shores of the Forth. With open views of the Forth and Lothian, the long and lonely range of the Lammermuir Hills forms the southern backdrop for this drive.

A curiosity to look for (located in fields, next to castles and churches and in gardens): *doocots* (Scots—dovecotes). Usually the free-standing ones are of Lectern type: rectangular in plan, with single-pitch roof. Beehive types are of circular plan and grow smaller towards the top. These ensured a supply of fresh meat in winter in the shape of squabs, or young pigeons, which could be lifted from the nesting compartments.

Leave Edinburgh by way of the A7. From Princes Street the sequence of roads is: The Bridges, Nicolson Street, and Clerk Street. At Newington turn left into East Preston Street, and right onto the A68, the Dalkeith Road, for Craigmillar Castle. The castle is reached by turning left into Craigmillar Castle Road.

CRAIGMILLAR CASTLE This is a magnificent 14th-century fortress associated with Mary, Queen of Scots, and managed today by the Scottish Office. Open daily throughout the year, the castle contains a stately range of apartments dating from the 16th and 17th centuries. Mary Stuart loved the commanding views of her capital city as seen from Craigmillar's embattled curtain walls, and in a room in the central tower she recuperated from the shock of the murder of her secretary and favourite, David Rizzio, in 1566. Here too, the murderers of Henry Darnley, Mary's second husband, plotted their foul deeds. The outbuildings of the castle include an interesting chapel.

Return to the A68, through Little France—so called because of the lodgings of the French servants of Mary Stuart

Craigmillar Castle

—and keeping to the A68 drive over the North Esk river at Lugton Bridge and up into Dalkeith. Your route through Dalkeith is: right at the traffic lights at High Street, sharp left at the next set of traffic lights, and follow the A68 out of Dalkeith, via South Street, Newmills Road and Lauder Road.

DALKEITH Once the centre of one of Scotland's most important grain markets, Dalkeith now plays its part in the electronics industry: ICL (International Computers Ltd) is based in Dalkeith House. If you have time to tarry look for the *East Church* (St Nicholas) in the High Street. This late medieval church, restored in 1852, contains the tombs of James Douglas, 1st Earl of Morton, and below the choir is the burying place of Anne, Duchess of Buccleuch, immortalised in Sir Walter Scott's long romantic poem *The Lay of the Last Minstrel* (1805). At the end of the High Street is *Dalkeith House,* rebuilt in the 18th century by James Smith, once the home of the Dukes of Buccleuch. Its grounds are now open to the public and contain an 'Adventure Trail'. In the High Street too, is the town's *Tolbooth* with pediment of 1648. *Note:* A 'Tolbooth' was the Scottish equivalent of the English 'town hall', and was a tax office which contained a burgh council chamber and a prison.

Keeping to the A68, make for Pathhead. Almost at Pathhead—just before the Thomas Telford bridge of 1827— look for the Stair Arms Hotel (it has a carriage in the gardens); opposite is the estate of Oxenfoord Castle, the home of the Dalrymples, the Earls of Stair. The castle is at present a private school. At Pathhead the A68 now becomes a single wide street for about half a mile, curving up-hill. The street is lined almost continually with single- and two-storey houses of the 18th to 20th centuries; note how the earlier roofs are of red pantiles and of steeper pitch. Pantiles, roof tiles of curved S-shaped section, came to Scotland in the Middle Ages as ballast from the Low Countries.

As you drive out of Pathhead look right (on the tree-lined side) for an unmarked minor road with a sign to Crichton Castle. The road is narrow, so care should be taken, but the views of the valley of the Tyne are very rewarding.

CRICHTON CASTLE Pronounced 'Cryton', this castle is open daily and is one of the most spectacularly sited castles in Scotland. It was built as a plain tower-house in the 14th century, but has additions of the 15th and 17th centuries. Perhaps the most startling feature is the Italianate wing added between 1581 and 1591 by the nephew of the rapacious Earl of Bothwell, Mary, Queen of Scots' third husband. The castle is associated with Sir Walter Scott's prose poem *Marmion* (1808) which describes the arcaded range thus:

> Still rises unimpaired below
> The courtyard's graceful portico
> Above its cornice, row and row
> Of fair hewn facets richly show
> Their pointed diamond form.

To the west of the village of Crichton is an early Iron Age fort, and the naveless collegiate church was built in 1449 for James II's ruthless Chancellor, Sir William Crichton.

From Crichton follow the signs for the B6372 and the Victorian mining village of Gorebridge. Follow the B6372 to skirt Temple, which takes its name from the Knights Templar (soldier knights whose purpose was to protect pilgrims on their journeyings to and from Jerusalem), who had an important base here.

At Gorebridge cross the A7 (Edinburgh/Galashiels road) and follow the B6372. There are many suitable sites hereabouts for picnics. This road will take you, via Rosebery and Mount Lothian, to join the A701 to Penicuik.

PENICUIK   Once a papermaking town, Penicuik was the site of the Scottish cotton industry which began here in 1778. On the left bank of the river North Esk, Penicuik has managed to retain its coal industry, and new industries have established themselves on the Eastfield Estate. The architectural influence of the Clerk family is still very evident in the town (particularly *St Mungo's Parish Church* of 1771) and *Penicuik House* — an ideal Scots Palladian house — is worthy of note.

Take the A701 out of Penicuik for some three miles; then turn right onto the B7003 for the mining village of Roslin.

ROSSLYN CASTLE   This was built in the 15th century by the Sinclair family, Earls of Caithness. Rosslyn Chapel was

Penicuik House

intended as a collegiate church and was founded in 1446 by William Sinclair. It was never finished and became a burial place of the Sinclairs, and is known today for its leafy 'Prentice Pillar'; this is said to have been carved by an apprentice during his master's absence. On his return the master was so jealous of the apprentice's work that he killed him. Scott commemorated the chapel in *The Lay of the Last Minstrel*.

From Roslin take the B7006 to its junction with the A701. Turn right for Straiton and Liberton. The following sequence of roads will bring you back to where you turned off onto the A68 (for Dalkeith): Liberton Gardens, Liberton Brae, Nether Liberton, Craigmillar Park, Mayfield Gardens, Minto Street and straight forward for Princes Street.

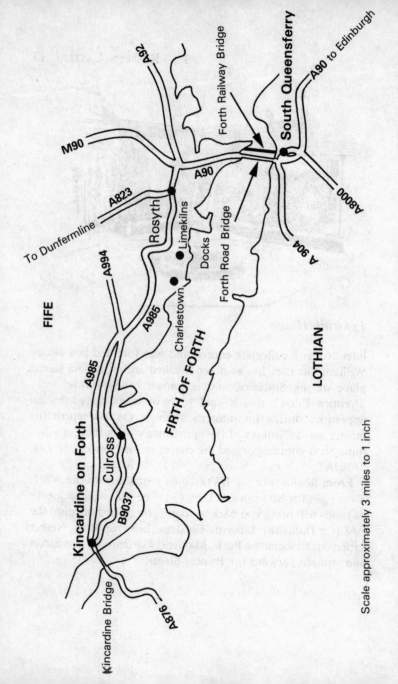

Scale approximately 3 miles to 1 inch

2 Edinburgh – Forth Road Bridge – Rosyth – Kincardine-on-Forth – Culross – Rosyth – Forth Road Bridge – Edinburgh (60 miles)

An effortless, enjoyable drive with excellent views of the Forth estuary, and plenty of opportunities to view the vital bridging of the Firth of Forth. A welter of Forth coast villages opens up, with street plans dating from the 16th century. All this combines to produce a scene that is without equal, and deserving of greater fame.

A curiosity to look for: mercat crosses (Scots – market crosses), erected in the Scottish burghs, generally in a wide thoroughfare, as the focus of market activity, or local ceremonial, or the punishment of offenders. Most examples are of post-Reformation date and have heraldic, or symbolic finials. They are not actually topped by crosses (too Papist for the Calvinist Reformers), but the name persists.

Leave Princes Street West and drive down Shandwick Place towards the Haymarket; follow the signs for the A90 and the Forth Road Bridge (toll charge).

FORTH ROAD BRIDGE   If you wish to look at the bridges more closely, just before you arrive at the road bridge look for the turn-off (left) for the motel (Forth Bridges Lodge), and drive into the car park. There is a viewing platform overlooking the Forth. Here is *South Queensferry*, an important ferry link with Fife (at North Queensferry) and the north since the time of King Malcolm Canmore's famous Saxon Queen Margaret who, in the 11th century, founded the great abbey of Dunfermline, abutting her husband's royal palace. Ferry boats continued to ply right up to the building of the *Forth Road Bridge*, which cost £20,000,000. This suspension bridge is 2415 yards long, and was opened by H.M. Queen Elizabeth II on 4th September 1964. To the east is the much-renowned *Forth Railway Bridge,* built in 1890, and some 2432 yards long. Below is *South Queensferry* with the ancient 'Hawes Inn', dating from 1683, which was featured in Sir Walter Scott's *The Antiquary* (1816) and Robert Louis Stevenson's *Kidnapped* (1886); this was the successor of a hospice for pilgrims (on their way to Dunfermline Abbey and St Andrews Cathedral), set up by Queen Margaret.

Once across the bridge and past the second escarpment on the left move into the left-hand lane of the A90 and look for the sliproad for Rosyth. Drive to the bottom of this sliproad and, at the roundabout, turn left into Rosyth, down the A985.

ROSYTH Built by the government in the early 1900s, Rosyth owes its importance to the Royal Navy Dockyard (open to the public on special Navy Days as announced in the press), which flourished during the two World Wars. The dockyard church has memorials of famous ships like the 'Mauritania,' broken up in 1935. Amid the expansive buildings needed for modern naval affairs stands the 16th-century Rosyth Castle, once the home of the Stewarts of Rosyth, and mentioned by Sir Walter Scott in his *The Abbot* (1820). In the heart of the 'garden city' of Rosyth lies the ground fought over by Cromwellian troops in 1651.

Follow the A985 out of Rosyth. To the left are the Forth coast villages of Charlestown and Limekilns, worth a visit if you have time for a detour. One of Charlestown's principal features is the old model 18th-century village with its green. At the foot of the cliff are the ancient limekilns built into the rock. The village of Limekilns was mentioned by Robert

Louis Stevenson in *Kidnapped*. The 17th-century Academy Square contains the 'King's Cellars', thought to have been a depository for the wine for Dunfermline Palace. Near the village is the 19th-century Broomhall House, the home of the Earls of Elgin, whose ancestor brought the Elgin Marbles, the sculptures from the frieze of the Parthenon, to the British Museum.

Follow the A985 to the roundabout at Cairneyhill; cross and follow the signs to Kincardine-on-Forth.

KINCARDINE-ON-FORTH Once a small seafaring centre, particularly noted for its boatbuilding, the town is now mainly a residential area for the Kincardine Power Station. Nearby is the police training college of Tulliallan Castle. Rest in the town for refreshments and look for the 17th-century *Mercat Cross* with the arms of the Earl of Kincardine. Sir John Dewar, who invented the vacuum flask, was born here in 1842. The town houses have an interesting array of carved date panels.

KINCARDINE BRIDGE Built in 1936, the half-mile long bridge spans the Forth and is the last crossing before the estuary widens; it has a central swing span of 100 yards and replaced an ancient ferry.

Turn right at the roundabout at the centre of Kincardine onto the A876. Take the next main turning right onto the B9037. Follow the road to Culross, one of Scotland's showplace towns.

CULROSS (pronounced Kew-ross) The 17th century was the golden age of Culross, the picturesque little Royal Burgh, and it has managed to retain its unspoiled nature because it is largely in the control of the National Trust for Scotland. During the 16th and 17th centuries Culross was a thriving community trading in coal and salt, and it was developed by a businesslike laird (Scotland's equivalent of the 'lord of the manor'), Sir George Bruce. Later Culross was known for its 'girdles', special pans for making oatcakes. Coal and salt from Culross were shipped to the continent, particularly Holland. The modern appearance of the burgh is largely due to the National Trust for Scotland (NTS), who have continually restored the buildings since the 1930s; their policy

Culross Palace

has been aimed at achieving modern living standards while preserving characteristic architecture.

The Palace: under the administration of the Scottish Office. This delightful mansion was built in 1597-1611 by Sir George Bruce of Culross, who was knighted by King James VI. The crow-stepped gables (sometimes called 'corbie-steps'), where the gable has stepped instead of sloping sides, and pantiled roofs have ever been a favourite subject for artists.

The painted ceilings are amongst the finest in Scotland; adjoining the palace is a terraced garden.

The Abbey: what is left of the Cistercian monastery, founded by Malcolm, Earl of Fife, 1217, was reconstructed in the reign of James IV, but a large part of the building dates from the 1300s with a nave wall of the early 1200s. The remains of the choir are used as a parish church, which preserves the rood screen and pulpitum. The fine central tower bears the arms of Abbot Masoun (1498-1513). This too, is administered by the Scottish Office.

The Town House (NTS) dates from 1626. *The 'Snuffmaker's' House* of 1673 carries the inscription: 'Who would have thocht it, noses would have bocht it.'

Bishop Leighton's Study: Bishop of Dunblane (he died in 1684), Leighton was known as a bibliophile. Now under the care of the NTS, the house has fine panelling.

St Mungo's Chapel: built in 1503 by Archbishop Blackadder on the traditional site of the Glasgow apostle's birthplace, the ruins were presented to the NTS by the Earl of Elgin in 1947.

Note: The NTS have audio-visual displays at Culross.

All this area has linked its modern fortunes with coalmining and the B9037 continues eastwards touching the coalfields of Valleyfield, Torryburn and the mining hamlets of Blairburn, Comrie and Shire's Mill. Continue on the B9037 where it meets the A985 and A994, and turning right follow the A985 to the A90 via Rosyth. The A90 leads directly back to Edinburgh across the Forth Road Bridge.

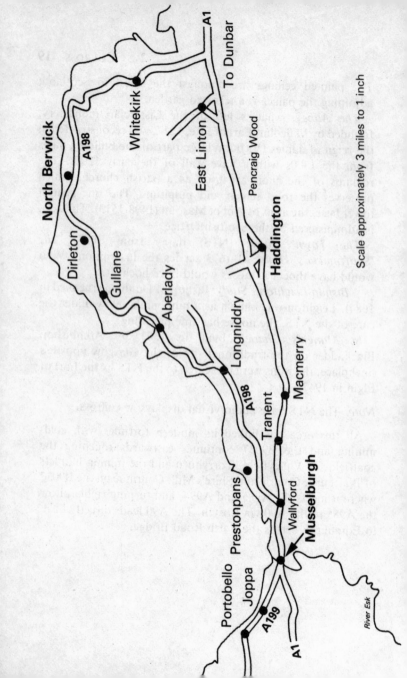

Scale approximately 3 miles to 1 inch

3 Edinburgh – Portobello – Joppa – Musselburgh – Tranent – Macmerry – Gladsmuir – Haddington – East Linton – Whitekirk – North Berwick – Dirleton – Gullane – Aberlady – Longniddry – Prestonpans – Musselburgh – A1 to Edinburgh (56 miles)

This drive traverses one of the most fertile of Scotland's areas, with its distinctive red soil. It opens up the mainly flat coastline, with its resorts largely devoted to golf. Picturesque views are offered of the haunts of sea birds.

A curiosity to look for (seen in farmyards): the conical pantiled roofs of the horse-mills. These are circular or polygonal farm buildings in which a central shaft, turned by a horse, supplied the driving force for agricultural machinery.

From the East End of Princes Street drive down Waterloo Place (the Calton Hill is high up on your left), and Regent Road to the junction between Montrose Terrace and London Road, where you turn right. At Jock's Lodge (the crossroads past the Meadowbank sports complex) drive straight forward down Portobello Road and at the major crossroads (there is a huge open area where the power station used to be) turn right into Portobello High Street (A199). This will take you through Portobello and Joppa to Eastfield, where the A199 joins the A1 (the Great North Road) for Musselburgh.

PORTOBELLO A popular seaside resort, with a marine promenade, named (it is said) by Admiral Edward Vernon after the site of his victory in Panama in 1739. Valuable clay deposits in the vicinity established the town's brick-making and pottery. This is the birthplace of Scotland's famous comedian, Sir Harry Lauder.

JOPPA This is the western extension of Portobello. Hereabouts were the salt pans which flourished when salt was needed to pack the barrels of herring.

MUSSELBURGH The town obtained its name from a mussel bank at the mouth of the river Esk; during your drive you pass over the Esk by way of John Rennie's bridge of 1806 (widened in 1924). There is a wide selection of interesting houses in the area, and where the High Street widens are the *Tolbooth* (1590) and *Loretto* private school, which now incorporates the 16th-century *Pinkie House*.

Out of Musselburgh, past the racecourse (on the left), follow the A1 to the Wallyford roundabout, over the main railway line to London. With the motel and filling-station on your left, drive up the hill and past Dolphingstone farm to Tranent.

TRANENT This has been a mining village since the 13th century. Here the A1 becomes Bridge Street and High Street, and there is an unbroken line of the traditional two-storey houses, punctuated by public houses. Modern Tranent has been geared to the commuter to and from Edinburgh. The original burgh lies downhill (on the left) towards the Forth, and can be examined at leisure for Kirk, War Memorial (which stands in for a mercat cross) and modern Civic Centre.

Continue on the A1 for 1¾m to Macmerry.

MACMERRY The village has long had its own air of independence, and now has a thriving local-authority industrial estate. As you pass through look to your left (past the post office) for the agreeable half-square of typical Scottish council houses dating from 1925.

A mile and a half along the road is Gladsmuir—once the haunt of highwaymen, preying on this main coach route to

Edinburgh — with its pantiled cottages. A little further on, the A1 will take you quickly along the northern edge of Haddington, but a visit to this historic Lothian town is recommended for the visitor with an hour or so to spare.

HADDINGTON A target for English raiders in the Middle Ages, Haddington has long been noted for its grain market and was a *Royal Burgh*. (As you travel the routes set out in this book you will come across three types of Burgh (*cf.* English 'borough'). A 'Royal Burgh' obtained its Charter from the Crown; a 'Burgh of Barony' was created by King or Baron; and a 'Police Burgh' was managed by commissioners.) The reformer John Knox (1505-72) is thought to have been born in or near Haddington.

The Town House: built in 1748, with its curfew bell (103 chimes), it was originally designed by William Adam.

Haddington House: a 17th-century town house restored in 1969.

The Mercat Cross: this is topped with the figure of a goat.

Haddington Church: the church was dedicated to St Mary and was extant in 1462; some say that it is the most impressive of the late medieval Scottish burgh kirks. Restored 1971-73, the church contains a number of interesting memorials and tombs, of which one is to Jane Welsh (1801-66), wife of Thomas Carlyle.

From Haddington the view from the A1 opens out to give views of the wide plain of the river Tyne (to the right). Before you descend the long hill to skirt East Linton, look left for the layby at Pencraig Wood. Here during the summer months an Information Caravan is parked, and the site commands spectacular views of the coast by Dunbar and the Lammermuir hills. Straight in front of the layby is Traprain Law, once topped by the capital 'city' of the tribe known as the Votadini, who harried the Roman legions as they advanced north to the Forth, and later lived more peaceably alongside them. At the foot nestles the fortress of Hailes

Castle, built for the Earls of Dunbar. James Hepburn, Earl of Bothwell and Lord Hailes—he married Mary, Queen of Scots—and his family charged a toll from every traveller hereabouts, for the main road was once down in the valley.

Down the hill, the A1 now bypasses East Linton, a small town of red whin and sandstone, once having its own Provost (the equivalent of England's Mayor) and Town Council. Nearby is Preston Mill, now run by the National Trust for Scotland, with its polygonal kiln, undershot wheel and working wooden machinery—well worth a detour.

Preston Mill

Where the East Coast railway line runs parallel to the road, look left for the A198 turn-off. Turn left and follow the signs for North Berwick. Immediately you are driving through the woodlands of Whitekirk and Tyninghame. To the right is Tyninghame House, belonging to the Earls of Haddington; down the Limetree Walk (to the right off the A198) is the preservation area named after the pioneer naturalist John Muir, who was born at nearby Dunbar in 1838. The trees of Tyninghame have been famous for over 250 years, ever since the 6th Earl of Haddington, the founder of the plantation of woodland in Scotland, planted them in 1705.

In the village of Whitekirk — known for its miracles of healing in the 13th-century church, which once belonged to Holyrood Abbey — follow the A198. Just past Auldhame farm you can turn right, if you wish, and visit moated Tantallon Castle on its headland. Like Hailes, Tantallon is in the hands of the Scottish Office, and the castle was probably built in the 14th century by William, first Earl of Douglas. This romantic stronghold is described in Sir Walter Scott's *Marmion.* Three miles away is North Berwick.

NORTH BERWICK This celebrated Royal Burgh, fishing village and North Sea resort was once the southern terminus for the pilgrim ships from the shrines at St Andrews cathedral, linking with the Fife port of Earlsferry. North Berwick was a prominent mercantile centre in an agricultural area; the modern harbour dates from 1887, and around are a goodly selection of villas and hotels, witness to the town's Victorian heyday. Look out to sea for Fidra island and its lighthouse, now a bird-sanctuary along with Eyebroughty, The Lamb and Craigleith. To the south of the town is North Berwick Law (613ft), a fine viewpoint, surmounted by a whalebone arch; near the top is a watch-tower of Napoleonic date. Look too, for the 350ft high BASS ROCK in the Firth of Forth. This famous landmark is steeped in Scotland's literature and history; once the site of a chapel, a fort and a prison, the Bass Rock is featured in Robert Louis Stevenson's stirring tale *Catriona* (1894).

If you wish to avoid the centre of North Berwick, turn left into St Baldred's Road, cross Law Road into Clifford Road, turn left then right into Station Road and left again into Dirleton Avenue, which is the A198.

Making for Gullane, the A198 skirts Dirleton and the ramparts of ruined 13th-century Dirleton Castle, the home of the Norman de Vaux family. Although the A198 now bypasses the centre of Dirleton, the tree-lined green and houses have much to draw the eye. Archerfield House, to the west of the village, later took the place of the castle. Three miles along the A198 you come to Gullane.

GULLANE   The world-famous Muirfield championship golf course, headquarters of the Hon. Company of Edinburgh Golfers (formed in 1744, it is the oldest golf club in the world — according to written evidence), is situated near Gullane. From the sandy shore at Gullane, Alan Breck made his exciting final escape in Robert Louis Stevenson's *Catriona.* Not far away are the remains of the 16th-century Saltcoats Castle with its ruined *doocot* (dovecote). From Gullane there are splendid views over the hills towards the Lomond and Ochil hills and the coast of Fife.

Continue on the A198, across Luffness Links; 16th-century Luffness Castle, built by Sir Patrick Hepburn and much altered in the 19th century, leads, in a mile or so, to Aberlady. This quiet holiday resort, with its colourful front gardens, has a motor museum at Myreton and a Nature Reserve on the east side of the bay. Drive straight on where the A198 turns left to Longniddry — near the flat, sandy, stony coast of Seton Sands — and you will pass Cockenzie Power Station (on the right) and the fishing village of Port Seton on your way to Prestonpans.

PRESTONPANS   In the 12th century, monks from Newbattle Abbey established the mining of the saltpans. The town remains in Scottish historic memory as the site of the memorable defeat of the Hanoverian general Sir John Cope by the army of Bonnie Prince Charlie in 1745. Sir Walter Scott stayed in the town as a boy, and much of the local knowledge he gained he put into his book *Waverley* (1814).

The road now takes you back to a roundabout at Musselburgh, from which the A1 route leads you back to Princes Street.

4 Edinburgh — Forth Road Bridge — Aberdour — Burntisland — Kinghorn — Kirkcaldy — East Wemyss — Methil — Leven — Largo — Elie — Largo — Windygates — Kirkcaldy — A90 to Edinburgh (96 miles)

Sometimes still known as the 'Kingdom of Fife', Fife presents the motor tourist with delightful old-world maritime burghs which grace the eastern shores of the Forth. An undulating, mostly fertile area, Fife also has an important coalfield which lies in the south-western sector of the county.

A curiosity to look for: tolbooths, the Scottish equivalent of the English Town Hall. These were the burgh tax offices, and they contained a council chamber and a prison. Of varying styles and period of architecture.

Look at drive 2 (page 15) for the directions out of Edinburgh to the Forth Road Bridge. Once you have crossed the bridge, watch out for the signs left for Kirkcaldy. At the junction of the A90/M90 use the sliproad to the left and at the roundabout (under the M90) turn right, then left onto the A92. Inverkeithing is on your right, and in approximately two miles you pass through Hillend and come to an industrial estate on your right, and the turn-off for Dalgety Bay. Dalgety Bay has beautiful vistas of the Forth, and it is now a residential area and the site of much industrial activity related to the oil industry. Across Dalgety Bay is the holy isle of Inchcolm, with its ruined 12th-century Augustinian Abbey (boat trips to the isle can be arranged from Aberdour and Burntisland).

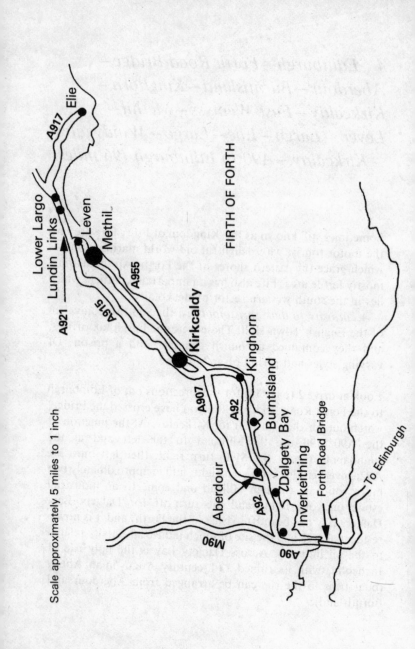

Scale approximately 5 miles to 1 inch

Elie
A917
Lower Largo
Leven
Lundin Links
Methil
A921
A955
A915
Kirkcaldy
A907
Kinghorn
A92
Burntisland
Dalgety Bay
Aberdour
A92
Inverkeithing
Forth Road Bridge
M90
A90
To Edinburgh

FIRTH OF FORTH

At the new roundabout (at the junction of the A987 and A92), drive forward along the A92 to the old Burgh of Aberdour.

Forth Road Bridge

ABERDOUR This holiday resort offers both peace and a variety of coastal charms. One of the town's showpieces is the 16th-century *Church of St Fillans,* rebuilt in 1826, described as 'a miniature cathedral'. Another historic gem is *Aberdour Castle* of 14th- to 16th-century architecture, the seat of the Douglas family. The town is remembered in the old ballad 'Sir Patrick Spens', whose hero sailed from the Firth of Forth to fetch Margaret ('The Maid of Norway') to be Queen of Scotland. Margaret died in Orkney in 1290, aged 7.

Continuing eastwards for about three miles along the A92, you come to the curiously-named Burntisland (pronounced as two words 'burnt island').

BURNTISLAND Once known for its shipbuilding and as a coaling port, legend has it that Burntisland—overlooked by the 632 ft Binn Hill—was an anchorage for the invading fleet of the Roman Emperor Agricola in AD83. Later the harbour was owned by the Abbey of Dunfermline and nearby *Rossend Castle* was also in their benefice. Mary, Queen of Scots, lodged at the castle in 1563—her courtier Pierre de Châtelard (he was in love with Mary) was found hidden in her bedroom, an offence for which he was brought to the block in St Andrews. *Burntisland Church* was built in 1592 to a Dutch design and contains a 'Sailors' Loft' and a 'Magistrates' Pew'. Characteristic houses are to be found in Somerville Street.

At Burntisland the A92 becomes Aberdour Road and Kinghorn Road; turn right at the roundabout. At the junction of the High Street and Kinghorn Road, turn left (into Kinghorn Road) and soon this becomes the A92 once more. As you drive along the foreshore, look out into the Forth for the once fortified Inchkeith Island with its lighthouse. If you are interested in monuments to royalty, detour, for a minute or two, right by the shore at Pettycur, for here a memorial marks a sad episode. On a stormy night in March 1286, Scotland's last Celtic King, Alexander III, fell to his death when his horse stumbled over the precipice.

On now to skirt Kinghorn with its views of the Forth. At one time Kinghorn was a prosperous spinning and ship-building centre, but now it has been developed as a residential area for the commuters of Kirkcaldy, and as an attractive tourist resort. The A92 now leads to Kirkcaldy.

KIRKCALDY   Well known for its manufacture of linoleum, Kirkcaldy was a Royal Burgh from 1450. Its boundaries have now stretched wide to enhance its name of *lang toun* ('long town'), and its main street is four miles long. The *Links Market* is a fair held here in spring, and is well fabled as the largest in Scotland.

Kirkcaldy is worth a half-day ramble to take in *Kirk Wynd* with its Gothic Renaissance style (1881), St Brycedale's Church, and many literary associations from John Buchan to

Adam Smith and Thomas Carlyle. Even if you cannot stop, look out for these things as you pass along the foreshore of Kirkcaldy: the A92 leads into *The Esplanade* — site of the aforementioned fair, recognised as an Eastern Chartered Fair in 1305 — built in 1922-23 to relieve unemployment; and thence to the High Street to pass the *Harbour*. Opposite the harbour is the golden-yellow-coloured *Sailors' Walk* (1459), probably once a prominent merchant's house. Here Charles II rested in 1650 on his way to be crowned at Scone, and the building is now a Customs House. Up the hill — called *The Path* — the A92 passes (left) Dunnicher House, built in 1692 by John Watson. Now named *Path House* (and restored by the Fife Health Board for use as a nurses' home) it stands proudly in juxtaposition to the monstrous council flats, a modern monument to urban tastelessness. Only a few yards further on (to the right) are *Ravenscraig Castle and Park*.

Built in the 1460s by James II as a defence against the English and the pirates who harried the Forth, the castle became the residence of the St Clairs and is now in the care of the Scottish Office. Sir Walter Scott gave the castle immortality in his poem *The Lay of the Last Minstrel:*

> O listen, listen, ladies gay,
> No haughty feat of arms I tell
> Soft is the note and sad the lay
> That mourns the lovely Rosabelle.

> Last night the gifted Seer did view
> A wet shroud swathed round ladye gay;
> Then stay thee, Fair, in Ravensheuch:
> Why cross the gloomy Firth today?

Incidentally, Rosabelle did ignore the Seer's advice and was drowned within sight of Ravenscraig Castle.

Follow the A92 (Dysart Road — Townhead — Normand Road — Wemyss Road) out of Kirkcaldy. Now you enter the coastal heartland of Fife's mining area, which stretches under the Forth. Coaltown of Wemyss leads to East Wemyss, and thence into Buckhaven, Methil and Leven. The development of the coalmines in the area has meant the spoliation of the beaches with colliery waste. Buckhaven — once depending on the fishing industry — now has its harbour almost filled in. Adjoining Buckhaven, Methil has become the seaport for these 'sister towns'. Industry has almost destroyed Leven's genteel residential past; the town originally developed as the nearest port to the royal palace of Falkland.

By Scoonie Park, the A955 joins the A915. Turn up the hill past the elevated cemetery along the A915. The coast road now leads along a fine stretch of the Leven golf links to Lundin Links, developed as a resort for golfers. At Lundin Links are Celtic 'Standing Stones', which once had religious significance. The A915 now descends to cross the Boghall Burn, and curves sharply to the 'Largoes' — the two villages of Kirkton of Largo (or Upper Largo) and Lower Largo. If you wish, make a detour to Lower Largo in search of relics of Alexander Selkirk, the 'inspiration' of Daniel Defoe's *Robinson Crusoe*. A statuette and plaque to Selkirk stands above the door of a house on the site of his birthplace in 1676.

Follow the A921 and at Balchrystie, turn left onto the A917 for Elie.

ELIE   As with several other small towns in the East Neuk of Fife, Elie combines a group of hamlets under the collective name of Elie-Earlsferry. Earlsferry, a Royal Burgh of great antiquity, is deemed to take its name from the boatmen who ferried Macduff across the Forth when he was fleeing from the fury of King Macbeth. Now a popular seaside resort, Elie is steeped in Scottish history. The pilgrim ferry from Lothian assured the town's prosperity from early medieval times, and in the late 19th and early 20th centuries Elie's famous golfing son, James Braid, was one of the winning triumvirate of Varden, Braid and Taylor, who dominated professional golf.

By way of the A917, Elie opens up the East Neuk coastline to the visitor: St Monance, Pittenweem, Anstruther and Crail are only a few miles along the coast from Elie.

The road back to Edinburgh is easily followed. The A917 leads into the A921: follow this to Leven, and proceed on the A915 to Windygates. Turn left at the traffic lights at Windygates—past the whisky distillery—and drive on to

Elie Harbour

Kirkcaldy on the A915. At the roundabout at the edge of Kirkcaldy, drive forward onto the B929, which links with the A955. Turn right at the B929/A955 junction and follow the road over the level crossing through Kirkcaldy by way of The Esplanade. At the end of The Esplanade is a roundabout (at the Dodge City supermarket, left); drive onto the A907, and follow the road past Cullaloe Reservoir (left) to the junction with the A92. The A92 will now take you back to the A90/M90 for Edinburgh.

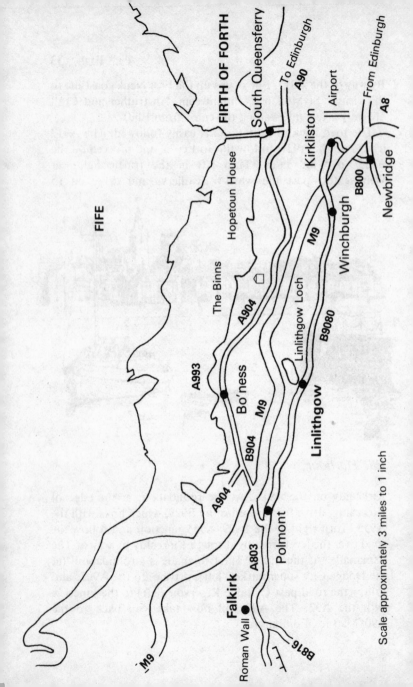

FIRTH OF FORTH

FIFE

South Queensferry

To Edinburgh

A90

Airport

From Edinburgh

A8

Kirkliston

B800

Newbridge

Hopetoun House

Winchburgh

M9

The Binns

A904

Linlithgow Loch

B9080

A993

Bo'ness

M9

Linlithgow

B904

A904

Polmont

A803

M9

Falkirk

Roman Wall

B816

Scale approximately 3 miles to 1 inch

5 Edinburgh — Newbridge — Kirkliston — Winchburgh — Linlithgow — Polmont — Falkirk — Roman Wall (Optional) — Bo'ness — Queensferry — Edinburgh (50 miles)

This drive offers sights which are less of scenic beauty than of architectural interest. It takes in the northern boundary of the flat shores of the Forth estuary, with its comparatively good farming land. A great deal of Roman activity took place in the western part of Lothian. The visible signs of the oil-shale industry somewhat mar the overall view.

A curiosity to look for: near Bridgeness Tower, at the east end of Bo'ness, is a copy of a Roman distance slab. It was set up in 1868 to mark the terminal point of the Antonine Wall. The original was excavated here and is now in the National Museum of Antiquities in Edinburgh.

The stone reads:

IMP CAES TITO AELIO
HADRI ANTONINO
AVG PIO P.P. LEG II
AUG PER M P IIID CLII
FEC

This is Roman shorthand for . . . Imperatori Caesari Tito Aelio Hadriano Antonino Augusto Pio Patri Patriae Legio Secunda Augusta per millia passuum Quatuor Sesquentos Quinguaginta Duo Fecit. Which means: To the Emperor Titus Aelius Hadrianus Antoninus Augustus Pius, father of his country, The Second Augusta Legion completed 4652 paces.

From Princes Street drive west towards Haymarket, following the traffic lanes signposted to the A8. Drive down Corstorphine Road and St John's Road, keeping to the A8. At Gogar the A8 becomes dual-carriageway—Edinburgh Airport is on your right—and you continue to the round-about. Following the signs for the A89, turn right onto the B800 for Newbridge and Kirkliston.

NEWBRIDGE The village has a crow-stepped, gabled inn of 1683; it is also the site of *Ingliston,* the permanent home of the annual Royal Highland Show. A local celebrity, Euphame McCalzean, was burned on Castle Hill, Edinburgh, in June 1591, for working witchcraft against King James VI.

KIRKLISTON Set on the River Almond, its 12th-century *Church* is worth a visit; it is particularly noted as the site of the tomb of Margaret Ross, the Countess of Stair (the stern Lady Ashton of Sir Walter Scott's *The Bride of Lammermoor,* 1819). Two miles west lies the 16th-century *Niddry Castle,* where Mary Queen of Scots spent her first night of freedom after escaping from Loch Leven Castle (in 1568), as described by Scott in *The Abbot. Newliston* mansion (1789) is by Robert Adam.

At Kirkliston, turn left onto the B9080, which soon passes under the M9 on its way to Winchburgh.

WINCHBURGH This is the centre of that part of Lothian laid waste by the oil-shale industry—now the shale 'bings' stand around as monuments to past prosperity. Look around for the severe lines of the Victorian brick miners' houses, with their gable brackets of red stone.

Follow the B9080 to Linlithgow. The Union Canal (1818-22) is on your right and you pass under it to enter Linlithgow.

LINLITHGOW Standing on the south shore of its own Loch, this ancient Royal Burgh was once the 'capital' of its own county, and known far and wide for its wells. Look out for . . .

The Palace: the birthplace of James V and his daughter Mary Queen of Scots, this was the site of a royal home for 800 years. Set above the shore of the loch, it is a fine example of a fortified palace with a spacious quadrangle. In 1646 the palace held the last meeting of the Scottish National Parliament. Prince Charles Edward Stuart stayed here in

St Michael's Church, Linlithgow

1745, and the palace was (perhaps accidentally) burned in 1746 by the troops of the Hanoverian general Henry Hawley. Today the palace is under the guardianship of the Scottish Office and is open to visitors at certain times.

St Michael's Church: rebuilt in the 15th century after a fire and 'restored' in the 19th century, this was the kirk for both townsfolk and courtiers. Showing marked French influence, the church was founded in 1242 by Bishop David de Bernham of St Andrews. Note the image of St Michael in the southeast buttress; this is the only 'popish image' to survive the Reformation. In the southerly chapel James IV had his vision of impending death at the Battle of Flodden, 1514.

At Linlithgow you meet the A803; bear left into High Street and Falkirk Road. Continue along the A803; bear left for Polmont and soon you enter Falkirk. (If you do not have time to visit Falkirk and the Roman Wall, turn right onto the B904 at Polmont. The route continues on page 40.)

FALKIRK   Once an important 'trysting place' for drovers — these were the men who herded the cattle for market — Falkirk won its industrial reputation with coalmining and the vast Carron iron works. As you pass down the High Street look left for the shop bearing the plaque commemorating Robert Burns' stay (at the 'Cross Keys') in 1787. Falkirk's *Town House* dates from 1813. The environs of Falkirk afford good views of the Ochil Hills and the rich vale of the Forth.

From the centre of Falkirk, drive west down Camelon Road and Main Street; before the A9 turn off for Stirling on the dual carriageway, and turn left onto the B816 for Bonnybridge. At Tamfourhill look for the signs for the Roman Wall.

THE ANTONINE WALL AT ROUGH CASTLE   The Scottish Development Department (DoE/Ancient Monuments) holds three sections of the Antonine Wall, along the B816. The best preserved of the Roman Forts — Rough Castle — is under the guardianship of the National Trust for Scotland.

The succession of military activities which culminated in the construction of the Antonine Wall by the Roman Governor of Britain, Lollius Urbicus, began immediately following the completion of Hadrian's Wall in Northumberland, in AD128. Hadrian's Wall was a frontier system designed to secure occupied Britain against hostile penetration from the northlands by the tribes opposed to Roman governance. The 75-mile long Hadrian's Wall stretched from the river Tyne to the Solway Firth. Yet the tribes living in what is modern Scotland exerted such a heavy pressure on the Roman garrisons on Hadrian's Wall that a new form of defence further north was soon deemed necessary.

Not long after Emperor Hadrian was succeeded by Antoninus Pius, the Roman soldiers on Hadrian's Wall reacted strongly to the hostile tribes by marching north to subdue and occupy the Scottish Lowlands, advancing as far as the Vale of Strathmore. Thereabouts they realised that the terrain made governance of the lands beyond the Forth difficult, but that territory they held in the Lowlands could be 'sandwiched' by building a new wall.

The Antonine Wall, which was completed, as a result of this decision, in AD142 or 143, extended 35 miles (some 39,726 Roman paces) from *Bodotria Aest.* (Bridgeness, Firth of Forth) to *Clota Fl.* (Old Kirkpatrick on the River Clyde) and formed a barrier over the narrowest part of Britain.

The defences of the wall comprised essentially a *ditch,* some 40 feet wide and 12 feet deep, backed by a *rampart* built for the most part by turf blocks and set upon a stone foundation around 14 feet broad. The Roman garrison of the wall occupied forts which were set up at the rear of the rampart and were linked by a military road.

The Antonine Wall never had the lasting effect of that of

Hadrian and soon after completion was evacuated. Some of the forts were later rebuilt, but the wall was overwhelmed by tribesmen from the north. The wall was finally abandoned before the end of the second century.

ROUGH CASTLE Covering approximately an acre, the fort, with its double ditches and annexe to the east, is one of the most notable Roman military sites in Britain. A feature to look out for is the series of defensive pits, *lilia,* outside the Antonine ditch. The fort was garrisoned by the soldiers known as the 6th Nervian Cohort.

From Falkirk, drive east back down the A803. At Polmont, turn left onto the B904. Soon you will cross the M9 and on your far left are vestiges of the Roman Wall and the site of the Roman Camp of Little Kerse. The road bears right and runs parallel to the site of the wall. At Inveravon the B904 becomes the A904, which you now follow to Bo'ness.

BO'NESS (a contraction of Borrowstounness) The town is industrial, with associations with the early history of steam-engineering. In 1764 James Watt experimented with his steam engine in nearby Kinneil estate, now a public park. Sixteenth-century *Kinneil House,* once the residence of the Scottish philosopher, Professor Dugald Stewart, is open on weekdays. The *Antonine Wall* had its Forth-end at Bridgeness in the eastern part of the modern town, with the back-up fort at Carriden House.

By Kinneil Park, on the edge of Bo'ness, turn right onto the A993 (as it passes through Maidenpark and Newtown the A993 follows exactly the line of the Roman Wall) and follow this to its junction with the A904 at Muirhouse. Turn onto the A904 and follow the road to Queensferry (see Drive 2) and thence back to Edinburgh. Along the A904 you will see signs off to the 'stately homes' of The Binns and Hopetoun House. If you have time pay them both a visit; they are open during the usual seasonal times.

The House of the Binns is the ancient home of the Dalyells. Parts of the house date from the 17th century and are fine examples of the transition in Scottish architecture from the fortified house to the mansion. There is a woodland walk here giving panoramic views of the Forth.

Hopetoun House was originally designed for the 1st Earl of Hopetoun by Sir William Bruce. Building began in 1699 and was completed in 1703; enlargements were made by William Adam from 1721. Interior decoration was carried on by Adam's sons Robert and John and can still be seen. It is presently the home of the 3rd Marquess of Linlithgow.

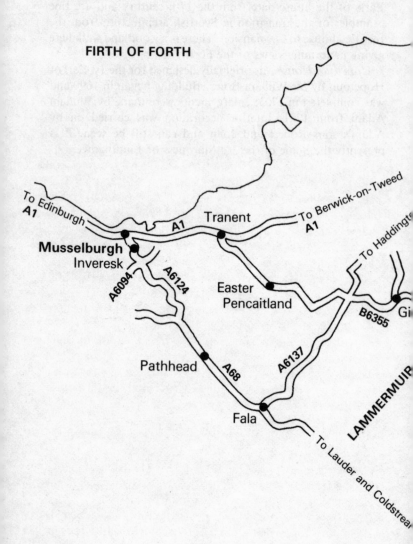

Scale approximately 4 miles to 1 inch

FIRTH OF FORTH

To Edinburgh
A1

Musselburgh
Inveresk

A6094

A6124

A1 Tranent

To Berwick-on-Tweed
A1

To Haddington

Easter
Pencaitland

B6355

Gi

Pathhead

A68

A6137

Fala

LAMMERMUIR

To Lauder and Coldstream

6 Edinburgh – Musselburgh – Inveresk – Carberry – Pathhead – Fala – Gifford – Easter Pencaitland – Tranent – Edinburgh (45 miles)

An attractive look at the by-roads and villages in the foothills of the Lammermuirs is offered by this drive. Agricultural scenery gives way to moorland vistas.

A curiosity to look for: the Scottish *Kirk* (church) can be looked at in all the drives. The medieval churches, abbeys and chapels of the Roman faith were turned into Calvinist meeting houses to hear the Gospels. Despite the spoliation of medieval churches by the Reformers, there was no sudden epidemic of church-building following the events of the 1550s; the medieval parish churches continued in use, and were modified, over subsequent centuries, to the new form of preaching which dispensed with the East-facing devotion of the Word made Flesh. Robert Burns was disgusted at the sight of new galleries and pews in the ancient naves and said: 'What a poor pimping business is a Presbyterian place of worship! – dirty, narrow and squalid, stuck in a corner of old popish grandeur . . .'

For the route from Princes Street to Musselburgh, see Drive 3 (page 21).

Once you have crossed the River Esk at Musselburgh, move into the right-hand lane and at the traffic lights turn right onto the A6124; this will take you into Inveresk.

INVERESK Now adjoining Musselburgh, the town is known for its papermills, and, to archaeologists, as the site of a Roman Fort. The *Parish Church* — set on a height from which the view ranges over a large extent of the country — dates from 1805. A mound in the churchyard is said to have served Cromwell as a battery site during the wars of the Commonwealth. *Inveresk Lodge Garden*, the garden of a 17th-century house, displays a range of plants, shrubs and roses, and is open to the public; it is under the care of the National Trust for Scotland.

Drive through Inveresk, over the East Coast railway line. At the crossroads (junction A6124/A6094) drive on, keeping to the A6124, and shortly you will come to Carberry Tower (on your left). Described as 'a baronial agglomeration', Carberry Tower was rebuilt in 1830, but retaining the old tower. The home of the Elphinstone family, it stands on the western slope of Carberry Hill, scene of Mary Queen of Scots' surrender to the Lords of the Congregation on 15 June 1567.

Keeping to the A6124 through Crossgatehall, join the A68 at Fordel Mains. Turn left along the A68 for Pathhead (see Drive 1, page 9, for details of Pathhead and environs), and follow this road to Fala. At Fala, turn left onto the B6457 for Humbie. In around 2 miles the B6457 meets the A6137; turn left onto this road and you will soon arrive at Humbie.

HUMBIE Situated at the foot of the northern slopes of the Lammermuir Hills, Humbie is known as a 'Children's Village', being associated with the Edinburgh Children's Holiday Fund of the early 1900s — the scattered Holiday Fund cottages are on an open site to the southeast of the village. Nearby is the 18th-century mansion of Johnstounburn. In the 18th century folk who suffered from skin diseases came here to take the acidulous spring water.

From Humbie drive on through this lovely vale to the crossroads at Bolton Muir Wood. There, turn right onto the B6355 and drive into Gifford.

GIFFORD This charming 18th-century village, retaining its *Mercat Cross* (1780) with its heraldically topped shaft, is

Gifford

situated on the Gifford Water with views of the Northern
slopes of the Lammermuir Hills. Gifford's *Church* dates from
1708. Southeast of the village, in its woodland setting by
Hopes Water, is *Yester House*, the home of the Marquesses
of Tweeddale. Ruined *Yester Castle* is best remembered for
its remarkable underground chamber known as 'Goblin Ha''

(Scots — 'hall'), dating from the 13th century. The chamber was deemed built 'with supernatural aid by Hugo de Yester, the warlock of Gifford'. Within the chamber King Alexander III had a mysterious encounter with an 'elfin knight', as recalled in Sir Walter Scott's *Marmion*.

From the centre of Gifford drive back along the B6355 across the Bolton Muir Wood crossroads for East Saltoun.

EAST SALTOUN   Once known as the first place in Britain to weave fine hollands (a variety of linen) and the first place in Scotland to produce pot barley, East Saltoun straggles, well-treed, uphill from its 19th-century *School House*. At the road junction an angel-topped *Fountain* welcomes people and dogs, as a memorial to John Fletcher of Saltoun (1903). The parish *Church* dates from 1805, and in its churchyard has an amazing profusion of 18th-century 'symbol' headstones showing skulls and crossbones, angels, bells and so on.

At East Saltoun follow the B6355 to skirt Easter Pencaitland, and drive down this road to Tranent to join the A1 for the return route to Edinburgh.

THE LAMMERMUIR HILLS   These windswept hills are popular walking country for those who appreciate solitude. They extend in an East-North-East direction from the vale of Gala Water to St Abb's Head on the North Sea. The chief summits are Meikle Says Law (1749 feet) and Lammer Law (1733 feet). Through these hills (descending to Fala) the Romans cut their Dere Street and the medieval pilgrims trekked to Holyrood and the shrines of St Margaret's Chapel (Edinburgh Castle), Dunfermline and St Andrews.

7 Edinburgh — Straiton — New Milton — Auchendinny — Howgate — Leadburn — Cowdenburn — Romanno Bridge — Halmyre Mains — Blythe Bridge — Elsrickle — Newbigging — Carnwath — Balerno (with Currie and Juniper Green) — Edinburgh (65 miles)

Views of the Pentland Hills are the keystones of this drive. Agricultural at first, dotted with industry, the route gives way to the moors and woodlands of Lyne. This was drover and outlaw country, which has, in part, changed little since the coaches of the 17th and 18th centuries were harried by highwaymen as they travelled from Lanark and Dumfries to Edinburgh.

Curiosities to see en route: moorland fauna and flora. Look particularly for the different types of heather and heath. The underlying soil of the hills is acid and often peaty. Cross-leaved heath has pink flowers and appears July-September. This is the time of year too, for the Bell Heather or Ling, of pink to crimson-purple; it grows alongside the purplish-pink heather in some areas.

Ravens, long-eared owls and red grouse inhabit the environs of this drive. The Scottish Blackfaced Sheep is a common inhabitant hereabouts.

From Princes Street (East End by the Post Office) drive south over Waverley Station following the signs for the A701. Your sequence of roads — all in a straight line — is: South Bridge;

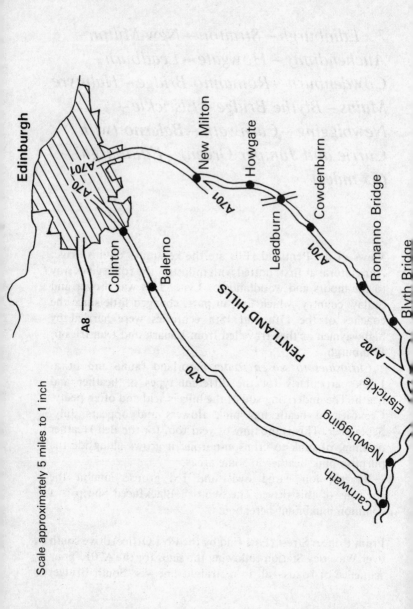

Scale approximately 5 miles to 1 inch

Edinburgh

A8

A70

A701

Colinton

Balerno

PENTLAND HILLS

A70

New Milton

A701

Leadburn

Howgate

Cowdenburn

A701

Romanno Bridge

Blyth Bridge

Eisickle

A702

Newbigging

Carnwath

Nicolson Street; Clerk Street; South Clerk Street; Newington Road; Minto Street; Mayfield Gardens; Craigmillar Park (here the A7 sweeps to the left into Gilmerton Road — *but keep on the A701*). Just past the junction with the A720, the A701 becomes a dual carriageway through Straiton. Pass the A768 to Loanhead on your left, after the dual carriageway. Watch ahead for the signs for New Milton and Auchendinny, and turn off the A701 onto the B7026.

AUCHENDINNY Known for the 18th-century residence — *Auchendinny House* — of the Scottish writer Henry Mackenzie (1745-1835), whose book 'The Man of Feeling' (still in print) so inspired Robert Burns. To the west is Penicuik (see Drive 1).

Drive down the B7026 and pick up the A6094 (south) for Howgate.

HOWGATE Famous in literature as the home of the carrier and his dog Rab, written about by Dr John Brown in *Rab and his friends*. Some four miles southeast, on the slopes of the Moorfoot hills, is *Gladhouse* reservoir.

A short way along the A6094 is Leadburn.

LEADBURN The village lies in a delightful moorland district in the foothills of the Moorfoots, which stretch out to the east to meet the Lammermuirs on the moor above Fala (see Drive 6). Blackhope Scar (2137 feet) tops the Moorfoots. The heather on the moor is burnt in rotation each year to promote the growth of the tender young shoots on which the red grouse feed.

At Leadburn rejoin the A701 for Cowdenburn, Halmyre Mains and Romanno Bridge.

ROMANNO BRIDGE Lying in the Lyne Water, the village is famous for its 'Romanno Terraces' (near Newlands Church), the relics of medieval cultivation terraces, known as strip lynchets. Down the Lyne Water, where it meets the Tarth Water (three miles away) is *Drochil Castle*, left unfinished in 1581 when its owner the Regent Moray was executed for his complicity in the murder of Mary Queen of Scots' second husband Henry Darnley. One mile northeast of Romanno Bridge is *Halmyre House*, ancient home of the Gordons.

From Romanno Bridge follow the A701 to Blyth Bridge. Look for the turn-off (right) for the A721 and Carnwath. You'll cross the A702 (Edinburgh/Biggar road) and come to Elsrickle and Newbigging and thence to Carnwath.

Carnwath Church

CARNWATH *Church:* only the aisle remains of the 15th-century church. *Mercat Cross:* bears road distances. The road out of Carnwath (A70) is known as the 'Lang Whang' and was much used by drovers. Some two miles north-west of Carnwath are remains of *Cowthally Castle*, once a stronghold of the Somerville family.

From Carnwath the route back to Edinburgh is straightforward all the way. Join the A70 (right at Carnwath) through the Pentland Hills.

PENTLAND HILLS Glorified by poets and writers, the undulating blue lines of the Pentlands stretch from Edinburgh's back door to the Clyde valley. Their average breadth is 4-6 miles, broken up by fine ravines, hollows and passes, the sources of many streams. The highest points are Carnethy (1890 feet) and Scald Law (1898 feet).

On the last part of the drive look for Balerno, Currie and Juniper Green — you pass through them all. Balerno is the last of a chain of villages linked by the Water of Leith, which skirts the northern slopes of the Pentlands. The village was once the centre of a local farming community. Currie was a small village centred on Edinburgh's 'town farms'. Juniper Green developed with an influx of specialist workers coming to the mills of the Leith Water. Spinning, paper and sawmills all added to the commerce of Leith Water. On its way back to Edinburgh, the A70 becomes Lanark Road and Slateford Road. At the end of Slateford Road, turn left into Ardmillan Terrace and right into Dalry Road for Haymarket. Drive straight on at Haymarket for Princes Street.

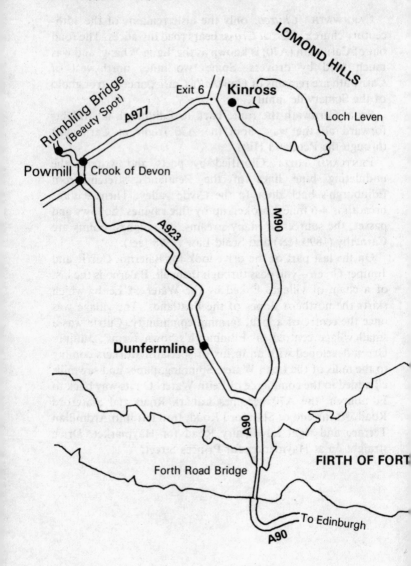

Scale approximately 3½ miles to 1 inch

LOMOND HILLS

Exit 6 **Kinross**

Loch Leven

Rumbling Bridge
(Beauty Spot)

A977

Powmill Crook of Devon

A923

M90

Dunfermline

A90

Forth Road Bridge

FIRTH OF FORT

To Edinburgh

A90

8 Edinburgh — M90 to Loch Leven (Kinross) — Crook of Devon — Powmill — Dunfermline — M90/A90 — Edinburgh (70 miles)

The most notable physical features of this drive are Loch Leven, the Lomond Hills and the Ochil Hills. It was an area once closely connected with the manufacture of woollens and linens. The picturesque gorges and waterfalls of the winding River Devon provide the southwestern part of the drive with its finest scenery. The whole is offset by attractive cottages, castles and the great Abbey of Dunfermline.

Curiosities to look for: not only on this drive, but on all the others, look for Scotland's curious stones. They may stand alone in fields — relics of Scotland's pagan religions — or grimace with faces at gable end of house and palace, or form part of a field wall. Some of them have carvings and scratchings of lovers long departed, of Roman soldiers and of tinkers showing the way to others of their kind . . . all adding to the mystery of the Scottish countryside.

For instructions on how to arrive at the Forth Road Bridge, see Drive 2 (page 15). Once over the Forth Road Bridge, the A90 becomes the M90; proceed through Fife and Kinross to Exit 6. Loch Leven and Kinross are on your right, backed by the Lomond Hills.

LOCH LEVEN This attractive *loch* (the Scottish equivalent of 'lake') is a Nature Reserve, famous for its pink-fleshed trout and its historic associations. The loch has two islands: *St Serf's*, with the remains of an old Augustinian Priory, and

Castle Island, with its ruined Loch Leven Castle. From this castle Mary Queen of Scots made her celebrated escape in 1568, after being imprisoned there for a year. Helped by William Douglas—who stole the castle keys—Mary escaped by boat; this famous story is told by Sir Walter Scott in his novel *The Abbot*. Loch Leven Castle, which is in the guardianship of the Scottish Office, can be visited by arrangement with local boatmen. To the east of the loch lie the LOMOND HILLS, Bishop Hill and West Lomond (1713 feet)

Loch Leven Castle

are prominent, with Benarty Hill (1167 feet) rising to the south. KINROSS, once the capital of the ancient small county of the same name, has its own *House* built by Sir William Bruce around 1685-92 (Bruce was famous for his work at Edinburgh's Holyroodhouse). The town also has a 17th-century *Tolbooth* repaired in 1771 and decorated by Robert Adam. On the carved *Town Cross* are the old *jougs* (a form of pillory once placed round the offender's neck as a punishment).

At Exit 6 turn off the M90 and make your way through this rich farmland to Crook of Devon.

CROOK OF DEVON This is the vale of the River Devon flowing southward through its picturesque defile. It makes a 'crook', or bend, here on its way to nearby Rumbling Bridge, a well known beauty spot. Away to the east rise the *Cleish* hills, with Dumglow at 1241 feet. A mile or so to the southeast is *Tullibole Castle*, which dates from 1608.

Drive forward on the A977 for Powmill. Then branch left onto the A823 which passes round the foot of Cult Hill (via Hill End) and Knock Hill — crossing the B914 — for Dunfermline. The A823 enters the town by way of Pilmuir Street.

DUNFERMLINE (Worthy of an hour's exploration on foot.) It could be said that the old Royal Burgh of Dunfermline is dominated by two 'kings' in their own right: Malcolm Canmore, King of Scotland 1058-93; and Andrew Carnegie, the industrialist. Some 1000 years ago Dunfermline was the capital of Scotland and King Malcolm built his castle in Pittencrieff Glen (now a public park, donated to the town by Andrew Carnegie). To this castle Malcolm brought his wife, the Saxon princess Margaret, who was to have such a major influence on the ecclesiastical history of Scotland.

The Abbey. This great Benedictine house was founded (1072) by Margaret. On the site of the abbey choir now stands the modern parish church (1817-22), which contains the grave of Robert Bruce — many of Scotland's kings and queens are buried here. Look (outside) the east end of the parish church for the remains of the Shrine to St Margaret, a holy place of pilgrimage for generations of Scots.

The Palace. This was the old gatehouse of the abbey which was reconstituted as a royal palace. Charles I was born here. Both the Palace and the west end of the Abbey are in the guardianship of the Department of the Environment.

Dunfermline was once famous for its linen industry, but more so for its 'most famous son', Andrew Carnegie, who was born in 1835 (the little cottage where he was born is preserved as a museum) in poor working-class circumstances. With his family he emigrated to America, and after early struggles he established the Carnegie Iron Works. He made munificent gifts to Free Libraries and other educational work in his home

Andrew Carnegie's house, Dunfermline

town. The Carnegie Trusts have made many gifts to Fife community projects as well as national charities.

Follow the A823 through Dunfermline (Pilmuir Street— High Street—New Row) and out via Bothwell Street and St Leonards Street. Drive on to the M90 and make for the Forth Road Bridge (follow the signs)—Dunfermline is 7½ miles from the bridge—and thence to Edinburgh.

9 Edinburgh — Newbridge — Kirkliston — Winchburgh — Linlithgow — Falkirk — Camelon — Larbert — Bannockburn (Battlefield optional) — St Ninian's — Causewayhead — Alloa — Clackmannan — Kincardine — Kincardine Bridge — M876/M9 — Edinburgh (80 miles)

The winding Forth estuary and the highest parts of the Ochil Hills, with the fertile, low-lying country below the range traversed by the serpentine wanderings of the River Devon, all give colour to this very 'historical' drive. All the symbolism of Scottish nationhood and independence is to be witnessed on this drive. The grass-covered Ochils extend along the whole northern border of the drive, with the highest point of Ben Cleugh (2300 feet) pointing to the delightful glens with the meeting points of tiny burns.

For directions — and details of towns and villages — on that part of this drive dealing with the Edinburgh to Falkirk section, see Drive 5 (pages 35-41).

Take the A803 out of Falkirk towards Camelon — the industrial village whose name calls to mind the 'Camelot' of King Arthur and his Knights — and at the end of the dual carriageway turn right onto the A9. Proceed through Larbert. Known for its ironworks, Larbert made guns used at the Battle of Waterloo (1815). Past Larbert, you cross the M876, but follow the signs for the A9 and Stirling, through Torwood and Plean. To the north are fine views of the Ochil hills and

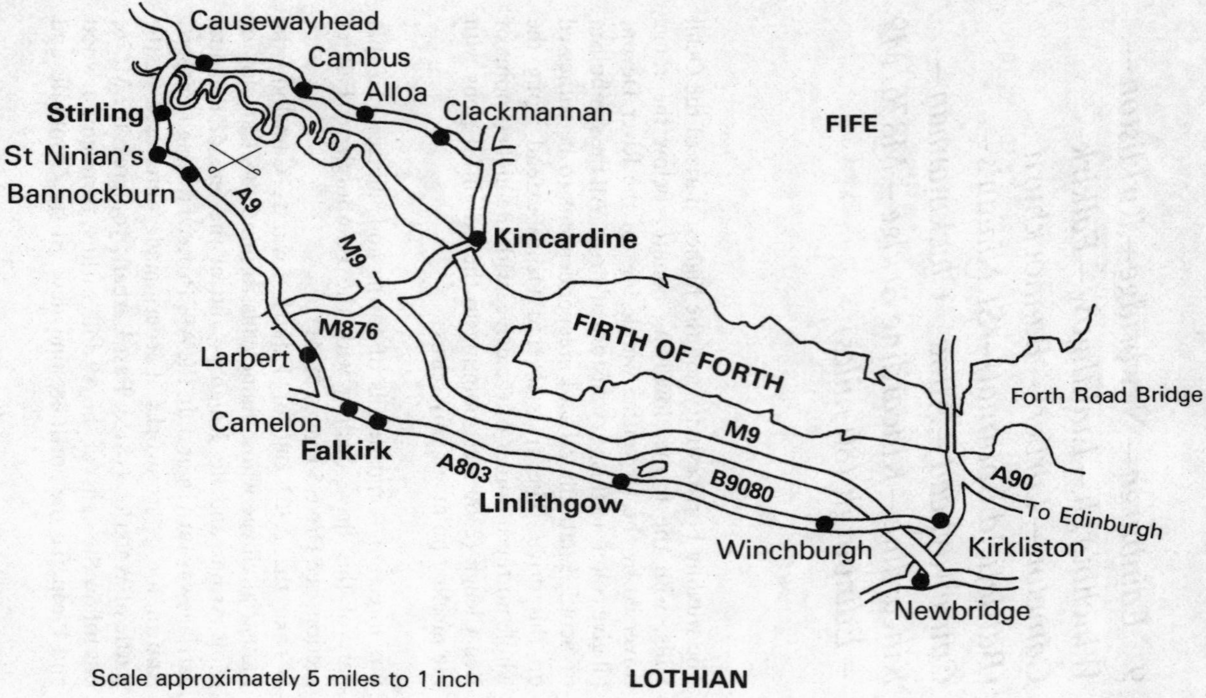

Forth Road Bridge

To Edinburgh

FIFE

A90

Kirkliston

Newbridge

M9

B9080

Winchburgh

FIRTH OF FORTH

Causewayhead

Cambus

Alloa

Clackmannan

Kincardine

Linlithgow

A803

LOTHIAN

Stirling

St Ninian's

Bannockburn

A9

M9

M876

Larbert

Camelon

Falkirk

Scale approximately 5 miles to 1 inch

the Wallace Monument (see below). Continue along the A9 till it becomes Bannockburn Road at St Ninian's, an old village now part of Stirling. If you wish to visit *Bannockburn* (see page 49), turn left onto the A80 and follow the signs for around three miles. If not, turn right and follow the A9 Inner Relief Road. At the next roundabout, keep to the A9, and at the New Bridge, cross over the River Forth and under the railway bridge into Causewayhead Road. At the junction in Causewayhead, turn right into Alloa Road following the signs for *Alloa/Clackmannan*. (Route directions continue on page 61).

STIRLING If possible, allow plenty of time to explore Stirling and Bannockburn. Long known as the 'Gateway to the Highlands', the history of this old Royal Burgh is closely linked with . . .

The Castle: this royal castle, set on a great basalt rock 250 feet high, was the strategic centre of Scotland. Looking down on the great and important battlefields of Scottish history, the castle was both palace and fortress, with buildings frequently destroyed and rebuilt. Today the castle still shows the architectural whims of its owners, such as the 15th-century hall of James III and the Chapel Royal, built by James VI for the christening of Prince Henry in 1594. The castle is in the care of the Scottish Office.

The Old Bridge: built in the Middle Ages, the four-arch bridge was rebuilt in 1749, after an arch had been blown up during the Rebellion of 1745, to stop the Jacobite Army of Charles Edward Stuart entering the town. Until the opening of Kincardine Bridge, Stirling was the last place that the River Forth could be crossed before the estuary widens. The battle of Stirling Bridge (1297), in which Sir William Wallace defeated the Earl of Surrey, is thought to have taken place near a now-vanished wooden bridge, a mile or so upstream.

The Wallace Monument: Sir William Wallace (1272-1305) was an outlawed Scottish knight who became the champion of Scottish independence in defiance of the English king Edward I, who had proclaimed himself Lord of Scotland. After being defeated at Falkirk, Wallace returned to his outlaw life, but was betrayed and executed in London. This memorial to him was erected in 1869 at a cost of £16,000. Standing near Causewayhead, off the A997, from the top the monument affords extensive views of the Forth and this part of Central Scotland.

In Stirling several 17th-century houses are still extant including *Argyle's Ludging* (a military hospital since 1799 and now a youth hostel) and *Darnley's House*, thought to be a nursery for James VI and his son Prince Henry.

Bruce monument, Bannockburn

BANNOCKBURN The battle of Bannockburn (24 June 1314) was the most decisive battle of the Scottish Wars of Independence. Edward II marched north with an army of around 20,000 men to relieve the English garrison in Stirling Castle. Robert Bruce, with an army of around 6000, blocked his way. Edward's vastly superior army was attacked and routed in their badly chosen position for battle. Thus was the seal set for Bruce's recovery of Scotland.

The National Trust for Scotland has a visitor centre, near the site of the battle, where audio-visual interpretations of the battle are available for visitors. Walks can be taken around the battlefield area where there is a memorial Rotunda and a fine equestrian statue of King Robert Bruce by Pilkington Jackson. At the Borestone, Bruce is said to have set up his flag. The site is run in partnership with the Scottish Tourist Board.

From Causewayhead follow the A907 to Alloa.

ALLOA Once this was the largest town in Scotland's smallest county—Clackmannanshire. It stands just north of the River Forth, with the long range of the Ochil hills in the background. The town was known for its spinning of worsted yarns, its brewing and its whisky distilling, and has a small harbour on the Forth. Nearby *Alloa Tower* was a stronghold of the Earls of Mar.

Enter Alloa by way of the A907. Follow Grånge Road (as the A907 becomes) into Bedford Place. Take second left into Bank Street and Mills Street. At the roundabout, take the third exit (Clackmannan Road) which leads to the A907 again. Drive on to Clackmannan.

CLACKMANNAN On the Black Devon River, the town has an old *Tolbooth* beside which stand the 'Ancient Stone of Manou' and the stepped *Town Cross*. *Clackmannan Tower* is a famous Scottish tower-house standing on its commanding site overlooking the town. It was begun in the 14th century and until 1772 was the home of the Bruce family. It is now in the guardianship of the Scottish Office.

Out of Clackmannan join the A977 for Kincardine. At Kincardine, cross the bridge and join the A876 to its junction with the M876. Drive on to the M876 as far as Exit 7, and join the M9(Edinburgh). The route is now M9 all the way back to its junction with the M8 near Kirkliston. Where the motorways meet, follow the signs east for Edinburgh.